How to Start Looking at Autism

Autism

Greg Stucky

Published by Greg Stucky, 2020.

HOW TO START LOOKING AT AUTISM

First edition. March 5, 2020.

ISBN: 979-8201438326

Written by Greg Stucky.

Also by Greg Stucky

Autism
How to Start Looking at Autism
How to Stop Looking Autistic

Philosophy
TL;DR Philosophy

Watch for more at https://stucky.tech.

Table of Contents

How to Start Looking at Autism

Greg Stucky

Other Books by this Author:

- How to Stop Looking Autistic

Websites by this Author:

- https://stucky.tech
- https://adequate.life
- https://gainedin.site
- https://theologos.site
- https://entertaining.space

To Adam, who took the risk to tell me what I needed to hear.

Why I'm Writing This

Autism guides are a prolific cottage industry, especially about autistic children. As a high functioning autistic, I find most of their information offensive.

Autism wasn't much of a diagnosis until relatively recently. Even though autism diagnosis is still a soft science, some profiteers have labeled it an epidemic. Autism Speaks says 1 in 59 children are "affected by autism" and that 50,000 of them transition to adulthood each year. However, most of the information describes *what* to do without explaining *why* or *how* ASD (Autism Spectrum Disorder) operates.

That information is surface level. If you want to treat how someone thinks, you must understand *how* they think. This book gives clear, simple-to-understand truths about ASD. While I don't have Dr. before my name, I'm a mid-functioning autistic who worked into high functioning, so I can see both sides of the issue.

The one takeaway I want you to glean from this book, more than anything else, is that ASD isn't really a "disorder". Now that I know how to wield it, autism has been one of my strongest assets. If someone with mid-functioning autism can withstand going to a concert, they can handle anything.

We need to start calling it AS, not ASD. 10% of the planet would be autistic if we could measure *everyone* on the spectrum. If we zoomed in on roles in STEM, history, writing, and accounting, that number would easily quadruple.

However, this doesn't mean that you can treat them like everyone else. I want you, the non-autistic (neurotypical, or NT), to understand in plain English who you're dealing with. While NTs usually need intimacy and affirmation, AS needs more boundaries than anything else.

The irony of AS is that it's risky for you to share the diagnosis with them. Far too many AS discover AS and focus strictly on their shortcomings and self-identify as a special needs victim. The only reason I succeeded was, ironically, because my family neglected to follow up with an autism diagnosis. The ASD identifier can only empower someone to become successful if they understand *both* their strengths and weaknesses.

I'm writing to neurotypicals who work or live around AS, along with anyone who suspects someone they know may have it. There's very little knowledge on AS. Far too often, you're either veering into the extremes of unnecessary harshness or unhealthy enabling. The "awareness campaigns" aren't helping much because it propagates the victim narrative.

By the end of this relatively short book, you'll have a heightened awareness of what autism is and how to approach autistics. I haven't seen this content discussed at length elsewhere, so this is my contribution to the discussion. Please use the ideas in these pages before any more AS resign themselves to inadequacy.

If you think you're autistic, I recommend my parallel book: *How to Stop Looking at Autism*. It's built with you in mind. For the rest of you, onward!

What Autism Is

Autism is now a buzzword. Movies and TV like *Rain Man*, *Extremely Loud and Incredibly Close*, and *Silicon Valley* clarify how autism looks. Unfortunately, visual media often fails to show how the mechanism of how autism thinks.

AS doesn't have any specific "tells". Most of them do, however, exhibit poor eye contact, sporadic behaviors, intelligence, and poor social skills.

AS thought processes run through separate pathways than neurotypicals (NT). The only way to gauge AS without being one is through experience imagining how they think.

AS is vague. I'm not kidding when I said that 10% of the population is likely AS! It's vague because science hasn't found many universal characteristics. We still don't see any formal AS testing for adults. Most of the therapies and treatments are intuitive guesstimates by professionals.

The following is my theory on autism's neurology. I've placed the web-searchable symptoms in **bold** for your convenience.

How Autistic Brains Work

This is the simplest "autism test" I know of. NTs see large letters and zoom down to the small ones. AS sees the small letters first, then build up their relationships into the large ones. Imagine seeing and thinking about *everything* that way.

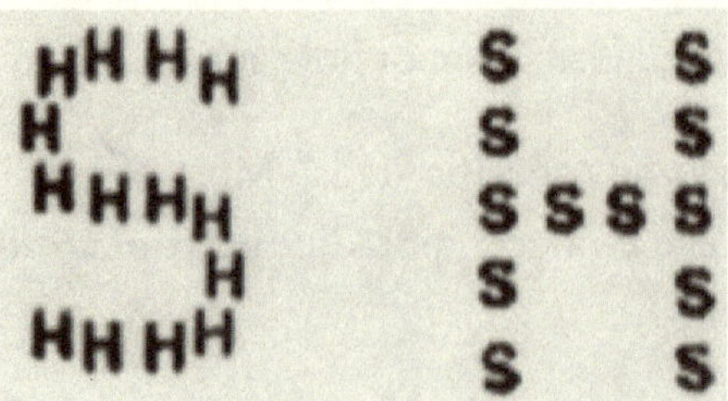

To paraphrase Temple Grandin, the autistic mind attends to details while the normal brain ignores them.

Humans start "chunking" from infancy. Chunking is grouping small things together as summarized larger things, then making patterns off it. For example, a baby will learn that 3 lines connected at the ends is a triangle and 4 is a square. Genetic or environmental factors will give a child **difficulty chunking things.**

Human brains receive a tidal wave of information, assign values to it, throw most of it away, then store copies of what's left. An AS child's poor chunking means they store more useless information. Their inability to rank information makes them **hypersensitive and/or insensitive to stimuli**. Too much information at once will overload them (also known as **over-stimulation**).

To cope with **stimming**, AS children often create fixed objects as "givens". Givens can be the order of things in a physical space, a familiar object, a certain method, or anything else that feels familiar. This over-attachment creates **over-stimulation when a given thing changes**.

AS people use behavioral coping mechanisms along with "givens". Most of them have **trouble making eye contact** because of how much information conveys through the eyes. They will often self-soothe with **repeating behaviors, activities or words**. They may focus on external givens like **spinning objects** or, in extreme situations, **self-harm**.

AS often battle **extreme anxiety** in interpersonal situations, mostly from trying to understand and meet expectations. That stress from managing the many social expectations creates a variety of **tics**.

AS escape the information overload with **sub-niche interests** (e.g., whales, 19th-century Scotch literature) with little interest in related subjects (e.g., dolphins, 17th-century British literature). The niche interest is a subconscious desire for a small, controllable world without an unmanageable deluge of details.

AS children can't "automate" thought well and **learn some subjects slower than other children**. When they learn, they'll develop an irregular pattern of competencies ("**splintering**"). Some of them have spectacular gifts (a "**savant**"). They'll also suffer **poor coordination** that could hamper their ability in athletics.

AS doesn't process feelings easily. Emotions are overwhelming for them, so their subconscious usually copes with **numbness to feelings**. Since they're generally ignoring their feelings, they usually have **trouble expressing feelings**.

Compulsive and impulsive behaviors are harder to resist without emotional awareness. AS are usually also **oblivious to others' feelings** or thoughts ("**mind-blindness**"). This unawareness may even go as far as **oblivious that others have differing viewpoints and presumptions**. This creates **frequent, consistent, inappropriate social experiences** and **trouble finding meaning in groups**.

Some of them understand challenging subjects while failing to grasp common-sense ideas. Their lack of common sense usually gets them in trouble with others. Anyone, not only AS, with a consistent record of failing at basic tasks would *naturally* battle **chronic depression**.

Scientists have sub-classed AS neurology into three major groups. **Visual thinkers** perfectly store and recall images. **Pattern thinkers** find connections between unrelated elements. **Verbal thinkers** masterfully manipulate language and words. Some AS can do more than one of these, but they all dominate with one of them. A visual thinker could be terrible at math or a verbal thinker might not be able to imagine a picture.

To broaden my theory into speculation, I believe AS battle the neurological issues of two-year-old children. They find mental workarounds that use completely different portions of the brain. The result is an intensely detail-oriented way of seeing everything. At its worst, they can *only* see the trees and not the forest!

AS Is Permanent, But Useful

There is no cure for autism. I must repeat. *THERE IS NO CURE FOR AUTISM!* Curing autism makes as much sense as curing bipolar disorder or ADD. Many people, especially concerned parents, treat AS as some sort of disease separate from the person. If you're a parent with AS, I've left an entire section at the end for you.

Accept the reality that an AS person will *always* be AS. They will endure tremendous emotional hardship and won't ever be "normal". While they have more weaknesses than the average person, every AS has more specialized talent than most neurotypicals.

At the same time, don't presume AS are some sort of Messiah sent to solve humanity's every problem. A rude autistic is a rude person. If they want to succeed, they need to learn manners. Throw my other book at any of them who might disagree: *How to Stop Looking Autistic.*

I began with my theory to give you a bird's-eye view of the diagnosis. If you don't want to read anymore, remember that AS is details, details, details. Autism lives and dies on intricate details. Give them more details, focus them on the right details, don't shy away from details, and never assume they noticed details.

The rest of this book gives concrete solutions on how to engage with autism's seemingly alien way of thinking. The infinite minutiae of AS means most of them aren't self-aware enough to tell you what I'm about to share, but most of them would agree.

Social Rules

Neurotypicals usually understand the importance of keeping a network and communication. Social skills are critical for human happiness, meaning, and success. Most NTs understand their networks as a component of their identity.

AS usually can't see the value of connecting with a community. That apathy means they don't often develop many social skills. By the time most of them realize its importance, they often feel far too behind to catch up. Many of them alienate themselves without realizing what they're doing.

Most high functioning AS adults believe nobody cares about their beliefs and thoughts. If they find steady work, many of them become hermits and find jobs with little human connection. Even if they prosper, most AS find ways to build emotional distance from most of society.

Some AS can thrive with social connections. They're uncommon, but the ones that channel their intelligence become industry leaders. You can recognize the high functioning AS by their eccentricity and intrinsically unconventional approach.

AS encounter most of their social problems because they don't easily grasp the nuances of managing a public image. Healthy social analysis considers what *appears to be* as much as what *is*, but AS usually only understand the facts they perceive without much regard to optics or narrative.

Conforming in society is honoring thousands of small rules. Some always apply (like managing hygiene) while others are high context (like signaling someone at a traffic intersection).

Most people are unaware of these rules but follow them out of habit. NT children grasp and emulate norms. These social rules become a series of telegraphed behaviors and responses that I call the "human interaction system", or HIS.

AS rarely prosper with the HIS because they either don't understand or can't remember to imitate the rules. Sometimes they'll imitate the rules when they're not called for, which is why high functioning AS are also often awkwardly polite.

Many AS don't believe the HIS will do them any good. The HIS always concerns itself with what people *ought* to do and rarely with what people *can* do. AS tend to like well-defined things. The vagaries and complexities of human engagement can often be overwhelming or annoying because they don't know how to make a "rule of thumb" on anything.

The HIS is inseparable from context. Subtle, profound differences in a few variables can redefine an entire story. AS doesn't usually know how to interpret these variables.

Here's a sample of the details a neurotypical may observe in a social exchange:

A hot dog vendor is selling his hot dogs when a man walks up with a swagger. When the man asks for a hot dog, he leans forward on the counter and speaks with a loud, demanding voice. The vendor's eyes dart around because of the public attention in the marketplace. In his anxiety, the vendor grimaces to show his disgust at the public spectacle and thrusts the hot dog at the man.

By contrast, here's what an AS may pick up:

A hot dog vendor is yelling "Fresh hot dogs here!" A man says, "One, please." He pays for the hot dog, then the vendor grimaces as he hands the man the hot dog.

AS tend to lack social intuition. Intuition is the ability to "feel" which details to focus on. While AS may be exceptional with details in their favorite things, the profound complexity of social patterns means they don't know *which* of the many details to pick up on.

Take the time to learn how an AS understands social interaction. They're far more rational than you may think. The trouble is that their logical connections fail to include common sense, so it comes across as child-like.

Here's an example from my life. When I was in high school, people would greet me with "hey, 'sup?" I would respond by telling them how my day had been. I took them literally because I hadn't been paying attention to how everyone *else* was responding. Then, when I noticed they were uncomfortable, I'd make the situation worse by assuming they wanted a more concise summary. I never *could* make a summary they were comfortable with!

Common sense is the set of prejudices one acquires by adulthood. AS don't have much common sense because they have a developmental re-ordering. They're not very skillful at assigning a general case from a method. They can learn it, but they're coming from a different culture entirely.

Anyone with two different backgrounds (e.g., international businessperson, cross-cultural missionary) is a "third culture" person. Third culture people never mesh with Culture A or Culture B because they're a combination of both. Even if they create change, they'll always stand out in their environment.

AS, especially mid-functioning, are third-culture. Since they're processing their environment in unusual ways, they're mixing their environment with off-beat conclusions that nobody else around them is inferring. Thus, they tend to form a culture of one.

Along the spectrum, mid-functioning AS are the most at-risk for unfulfilled potential. Low functioning AS have extreme challenges with staying in a crowded room and high functioning can often live a meaningful life without ever getting diagnosed. Mid-functioning AS, though, are awkward enough that society will shun them but have everything necessary to climb out of the social disgrace.

Awareness won't help this either. If I went to Russia, everyone would expect me to speak Russian. I could assert that everyone else should speak English, but I wouldn't connect with most Russians. I could connect with other English speakers who refused to learn Russian. We could make an awareness campaign to encourage everyone to learn English. When nobody responded well, we'd victimize ourselves and blame genetics. If some people started believing vaccines caused people to speak English, we'd have a direct comparison to today's "autism awareness".

Mid-functioning AS must remove their tendency to impress on others that they're "weird" or "odd". To make it happen, they must *want* to change. AS are responsible for their behaviors, but most awareness campaigns fail to address that fact.

Even when AS wish to change, most of them are frustrated by how poor the feedback system is in HIS. It's usually rude to confront others' rudeness. If nobody tells them, they can't have known! Most of the time, any reputations AS make can get lost instantly through gossip.

To the degree they're willing to hear it, address *every* concern you have to an AS. While you don't need to publicly confront them, specify exactly what boundaries they've crossed. Often, what you think is a rotten attitude is obliviousness to how rude or insensitive they sounded.

Most NTs manage trust with a sophisticated system of allegiances and appearances. You don't let strangers into your home, especially if they don't know you. But, if a stranger wore a uniform, said they were from the electric company, and showed you an ID card, you'd probably let them in. Trustworthiness is a convergence of intuition, common sense, knowledge, and reputation. We also understand that we can trust and be trusted at different levels.

Before they can learn otherwise, AS apply trust far more simply, a bit like a child. You're either "trustworthy" or "untrustworthy". They usually say things with no ill intent and presume you are "trustworthy".

Sadly, many of them reach adulthood embittered from many misunderstandings and exploitations of that trust. For them, most people are "untrustworthy" by default. The most insufferable bureaucrats and managers are high-enough-functioning AS to gain their position, then make everyone else reap their vengeance.

Many AS follow a miserable vicious cycle. First, they misunderstand something. Their misunderstanding leads to a response that'd almost be acceptable if they had understood the situation correctly. Then, people react from that out-of-place behavior. Most AS will internalize that trauma without learning the right lesson. Then, repeat at the next misunderstanding with more bitterness.

To break the cycle with AS you know, presume they had the right intent with awful skills managing it. If they know you care, they're more likely to want to change. Everything else comes off that.

AS Culture

AS personalities range wildly. But, despite their broad range of identities and dispositions, they tend to have a similar range along Hofstede's cultural dimensions.

Power Distance is the way cultures handle inequality. AS won't respect power tied to social structures that they didn't observe. However, most of them will adapt if you explain how to behave and why, even with high power distance cultures.

Individualism vs. Collectivism is the culture's focus on "I" versus "us". Since AS has varying degrees of "mind-blindness" they can't imagine what others are thinking. That obliviousness extends to unawareness of factors influencing a group. While AS are individualistic, their loyalty makes them a natural team player toward a clear purpose.

Masculinity vs. Femininity is the demarcation between a culture's focus on achievement, competition, and materialism versus teamwork, harmony, and empathy. AS exist everywhere on this dimension, but their personalities draw more toward masculinity.

Uncertainty Avoidance is a culture's willingness to try new things. AS hates new things that don't fit into predetermined expectations. By contrast, AS plows through convention when they're passionate about something. They're both more risk-averse and far bolder.

Long-Term vs. Short-Term Orientation is a culture's tendency to look long-term in tradition, custom, and the far future or short-term in innovation and the near future. AS tend to have a short-term focus on *everything*. Most of them must learn how to do things they don't want to do. While they can train long-term thinking, it's not common.

Indulgence vs. Restraint is the fight between satisfying or refraining from an urge. AS often have such overwhelming feelings that they follow their desires. Stopping an AS' desire is far less effective than redirecting it. Successful AS learn restraint only to fulfill long-term indulgence.

They Will Disagree

Many adult AS are offended at the need to conform. Why "lie" to others about what you are? Why deceive everyone to "fit in"? What right does the rest of society have determining what you can and can't do with your own body?

I spent years wrestling with that conflict myself. I couldn't grasp how the world measured value by others' opinions more than what was right in front of their faces. I kept cycling through jobs and burning opportunities through offensive behavior and unwillingness to do what I thought was "compromising". Nobody told me that value is a philosophical construct of the human mind.

All AS must understand that what you know isn't as important as how you make people feel. Everyone needs, more than anything else, to feel important. By their nature, all AS are smarter about specific niche subjects than NTs. Smart people must work harder than normal people to make others feel important.

AS is a culture that needs integration, not a sickness that needs a prescription. Society marginalizes many of them. They often disrespect without realizing it. Unless you can respect them first, they'll have no incentive to listen to you.

This is much more difficult than it sounds. AS are intense by nature and addressing an AS gives you their full attention. Further, most AS are in a survival state of mind from past trauma.

You must be patient with AS. AS requires you to think completely backward from how you see the world. Their views have profound insight if you can learn to decipher their way of thinking, but it's hard to believe that someone that awkward has sense in themselves.

AS Must Change

Social skills will always be a second language to AS. They'll never understand social rules well enough to be "normal". If they can fulfill about 85% of the HIS rules, society will label them "eccentric". At 90%, most people won't know that someone is AS. By my estimation, mid-functioning AS hits 60-80% of the HIS rules without trying.

AS have a single-minded passion. This passion will *always* form itself into some sort of obsession. They will devote their essence to a discipline, hobby, pattern or job. It can be harmless (e.g., Doctor Who), dangerous (e.g., watching violence), or even helpful (e.g., computers).

You'll know when you've found the interests of an AS because they won't shift from it. If you've ever been stuck in a conversation with someone about Yu-Gi-Oh, bottle rockets, automobile aerodynamics or agribusiness that feels strangely one-sided and profoundly informative, you've been subjected to an AS interest.

You won't be able to shift or obstruct their obsession much. They're more creative than they look and will find a workaround to bring the conversation back. Instead, try to discuss another related obsession. If they're into EVE Online, guide them to economics. If they like Star Wars, discuss the concept of spirituality or politics. A biology obsession can move to how taxonomies classify. A video game obsession can expand to sports.

An AS interest runs deep. AS children are often called "little professors" because of how well-read they are on subjects, but this brilliance is constrained to their preferences. If you shift the subject slightly, don't be surprised if they're completely oblivious to everyday trivia on that subject.

AS always has a topical way of observing the world, but it's one of their greatest strengths. That focus allows people to build elaborate and intricate things that NTs wouldn't *dream* of building.

AS must, however, understand the importance of social skills. The easiest way for them to discovered it is through their obsession. They're among the top 10% most knowledgeable people on the planet about whatever thing they're into, so they must expand that expertise into another realm.

AS must conform to the rules society gives them. The only way to inspire that mode of thought is through building an analogy for them. Often, they'll understand that immediately where they won't understand common sense. Here are a few examples:

- Biology: humans are a species that need investigating.
- Video games: life is a game with rules and objectives.
- Movies/TV: life is a very long movie or show.
- Star Wars: relationships are the Force that connects everything and brings unseen changes.
- Drawing/painting: conversations are a painting by multiple people on the canvas of time.
- LEGOs/robots: relationships are a brick-by-brick structure or schematic.
- Music: communication is a song with many players.
- Chemistry: human interactions are reactions and behaviors are catalysts.
- Computer networking: people are independent nodes with unreliable channels and conflicting protocols.

On a personal note, I visualize people as complicated computers with ridiculous subroutines. I borrow from my accounting background by seeing social skills as a type of asset management. I used to view everything as a video game but only apply that to tasks now. An AS who shifts through interests will naturally flesh themselves out as they grow.

AS is so detail-oriented that they don't naturally form common sense. Whenever possible, try to give them common sense by communicating how a specific instance can apply as a general case. AS can always handle the truth, but never a lie.

Because of the way AS store memories, they have crystal-clear recollections of events. New knowledge often gives us perspective in hindsight, so many AS will get stimmed when they learn something new from all the retroactive effects it'll create. This will ring especially true for social faux pas that you reveal to them. Adult AS have usually suffered many large-scale losses, wasted time, and lost opportunities from things they couldn't have known.

Since most AS have trouble with feelings, shame and guilt are overwhelming for them. While AS need counsel about social skills, they also need people to help them unpack feelings. If you're their guardian or mentor, your role as a cheerleader is critical. If you're a friend, you can't be half-in with them.

In Conversation with Them

Each AS is unique. You can't make a general assumption about one of them that can expand to all the rest. However, they all share a few patterns in conversations.

AS tend to take words very literally. If you say something will take a minute, expect them to get angry if it takes ten minutes. Only ask how their day was if you want to hear how their day went. Don't expect them to follow figures of speech or metaphors. Avoid any sarcasm.

Don't expect them to understand social context. They'll often say taboo things that would have been appropriate elsewhere. They likely won't notice subtle body language or changes in how someone says words. This vague understanding of social issues will extend to their sense of humor as well. Often, social interaction is ridiculous to them, which you may feel is inappropriate when they're laughing.

AS usually go their whole life not observing most common sense. Even when they're well-behaved, never presume they'll recognize subtle cues. If an AS is asking a question, they want to know and aren't trying to offend or patronize. If you're unfamiliar with AS, the questions will feel intentionally provocative.

AS are authentic, likely more than any other people group. They can be very forthright. Even when they know how to circumvent harsh topics, they always speak with a directness and intensity. That intensity mixes with many, many details. Though most AS aren't gentle, they're rarely malicious.

AS must cherry-pick from a wall of information to even speak. Most of the time, they focus so much on certain details that they miss critical ones. Don't expect them to recall important details. You might need to hear them speak in a roundabout way to get to the point.

AS tend to remember things for decades. They also tend to recall *exactly* what you said. This memory doesn't fade as quickly as neurotypicals, either.

AS are almost always loyal and principled, though it's often subconscious. They're dependable with clear boundaries, but vagueness evades them. Their loyalty also means they have a *much* harder time forgiving betrayal than NTs.

AS are self-disciplined to a fault toward their desires. While some may seem lazy, they're usually just unmotivated. Unlike NTs who learn how to appear disciplined, AS tend to forget how others see them, so they're often more industrious and virtuous than they look.

Successful AS turn public expressions, mannerisms, reactions, and body language into a performance. Some of them have performed habits so long that they look half-NT!

You don't need to understand AS to accept them, but your understanding can go a long way to respecting them. If you know a relatively normal-looking AS, they've likely had to work hard to get there.

Conflicts With AS

Conflicts with AS often become arguments in public. Don't expect subtle politics from most of them. Most of them have a feverish passion to "set things right" to their rigid understanding of the world.

AS must conform to many social rules that make no sense to them, so they're usually facing at least a few emotional battles at once. Since social skills are difficult for AS, they're all introverts. Skillful AS, though, may appear to be extroverts.

While every AS is creative, they need very clear rules. If you manage or parent an AS, you must give them motivation to both discover *and* follow social rules.

The poor common sense of AS requires them to constantly shift their understanding of the world. Most of them give up, but successful AS keep trying new theories until they find one that works. Most AS find it draining and become embittered, discouraged or depressed. Most of them must endure not understanding the world, and there's no quick or simple solution for it. All you can do is give them grace and respect their effort.

Discouragement

Any non-high functioning AS who reaches adulthood will usually become disheartened. They will either disbelieve their ability to handle reality or believe they have little value of working to fit into society. This discouragement, when taken to its extreme, is depressive bordering on suicidal. For about four years of my adult life, I'd battle an existential crisis about once a week. Further, the lack of skill in engaging with others can compound to make them more antisocial.

If an AS grew up in a very dysfunctional home, they're usually extremely bitter. Be careful around them. Depending on their life stage, they may antagonize you to conform you to their predetermined view of the world.

More than anything else, openly tell every AS what you legitimately think. They can usually tell that you're trying to hide or obstruct your feelings. While most NTs are afraid of losing a relationship, many AS will sever ties with anyone who isn't blunt with them.

To encourage them, give them *more* information, not less. They need hope they can succeed, and you can give it with your perspective. Even though they often have a cynical view of the world, resist the temptation to invalidate their views. Instead, tell them about positives alongside the negatives. More than anything, most AS must learn gratitude.

Disagreements

AS usually over-simplify things. They often have rigid presumptions that don't give room for shades of gray or uncertainties. Some of them will even honor their own elaborate code that doesn't connect with reality.

One of your most frustrating challenges will be when you must correct them on their beliefs. Many of them spend countless hours obsessed with hobbies that have fixed rules, regulations, criteria, and constraints. The world is far less defined than special interests and most AS have a hard time adapting beyond their scope of knowledge. They need patience, so try to see things from their point of view.

AS often have a disproportionate understanding of social severity. Many of them worry themselves over a minor slight, then brush off social suicide later. Give them context about what the consequences of their actions look like and explain what you can about why everyone honors those standards.

An argument with an AS is extremely draining. They'll often persist with their beliefs with an unwillingness to consider another perspective. At that point, they're passionate about that belief to where they won't listen to reason.

Talking an AS down from their anger is nearly impossible. Give time for them to cool off, think things through, and calm down. People often say things they don't mean when angry, but AS will often conform their beliefs to match it. Only make a threat with an AS you can deliver, or you'll lose all respect from them when they invariably test it.

Stimming

Neurological over-stimulation, or stimming, is the most ubiquitous public association to AS. The AS will rock, bark, yell, flap their hands, stare off into space or any other variety of odd behavior. They're usually unaware of their ritual.

Stimming is when the sensations are running faster than the brain can process them. Their brain initiates a fight-or-flight reaction to remove the environmental factors.

NTs can understand most other experiences AS endure, but stimming is far more difficult for you to understand. In my opinion, it's the worst part of AS. The best comparison I can draw is for you to imagine standing in a room. Then, put a blindfold on one eye, turn the heater on full blast, blow a warehouse fan in your face, add bright strobe lights, and play 15 songs from different genres at full volume.

Stimming AS need their minds to settle down. Most of them need physical space, but some with abandonment issues stim from distance. Most of them need silence, but if they're aware of their public shame they might need affirmations and positive communication. Your only solution is to observe their personality and respect what they seem to signal. It also never hurts to ask what they'd prefer.

AS often use coping mechanisms to stave off stimming. They're fighting a stim episode whenever you see them spinning something, absentmindedly handling an object, staring off into space or compulsively holding onto something. AS also usually create suppressed rituals to "cool off" like going to the bathroom, pulling out their phone or "scripting" by quoting exact phrases or words with no context.

Don't judge a stimming AS. To get a low functioning or mid-functioning AS to stop doing something mid-stim, command them to go elsewhere or do something else. That command will give them something to focus on. Stimming AS *never* need a hug or more discussion. The hug will give more sensory input and the discussion will create more uncertainty.

Dumb Rules

From an AS point of view, this world makes very little sense. The most influential people are the best sellers, not the best qualified. Leaders of analytical professions like accounting or science *still* need gargantuan political efforts to succeed. Even though friends are as temporary as our interests, we need them for wellness. The only constant to reality is change, but society seems to resist it.

Most AS get tied up on specific issues. Maybe they don't like the concept of tipping or can't stand how people don't reply to their messages. They'll focus on the frustration of certain details and neglect the broader picture.

Honor their unique perspective and empathize with how it doesn't make sense. You know how to ignore discrepancies in society, but they must learn that skill. You'll often discover they usually must abdicate a profound reality to conform to society.

They're Not Victims

AS are one of the most over-victimized classes of society. Many mid-functioning AS expect society to owe them something from their self-identification. Unfortunately, they often can't verbalize what they want!

"Autism awareness" campaigns don't help the situation. AS must integrate with society. Awareness *about* autism is important, but we also must expand awareness *for* autistics.

Inappropriate behavior is always unacceptable. Society should give grace to people who don't honor social rules, but everyone should at least *try* to honor the rules that were made for harmonious coexistence. Many AS are unaware of these implicit arrangements and need to be taught. To accommodate them is to damage society at large. Let's raise *their* awareness!

AS have a neurology that can endure rigors the average mind would run out of patience over. Many of them are also usually gifted. Many, many famous people are AS. If you look for it, you'll find them everywhere. All they need is knowledge about how to sell their thoughts.

There's a humanitarian reason for all this beyond merely "getting along". Their unique makeup means they can easily solve society's problems. One of them will be the engineer that solves the world's food or energy crisis. Another one will invent an algorithm to make the internet faster. The only barrier to their success is their ability to connect with people.

For AS to connect with the rest of the world beyond their niche, they need social skills. Thankfully, social skills are completely trainable, but only to people who want to learn. AS must believe their efforts are worth it.

You Won't Hear About Their Success

The irony of AS succeeding is that you won't know about it. High functioning AS become CFOs, CEOs, Senators, and Vice Presidents. Once you have enough experience around AS, you'll be able to spot that unusual mix of talent, suppressed quirkiness, and general disregard for common sense.

In fact, many high functioning AS aren't even aware they have it! Many of them are so busy succeeding without thinking about it that it doesn't really change anything for them. Further, their closest confidants and associates often forget. In my life, my wife frequently doesn't remember I have autism.

Any AS can find success. They need willpower, a supportive network, and time. Overcoming will make them focused, regimented, determined, straightforward, and analytical. From there, the only way is up.

Epilogue: Parenting AS Children

If you have an AS child or think it's a possibility, I imagine you've scoured the internet for answers. I hope this section gives solutions on how to support and empower your child. I added this here by popular demand, but I hesitate because I haven't tested most of these theories. I haven't brought my own children from birth through adulthood yet and came from an awful brood, but people seem to care what I believe.

Above all, try to not compare your AS child with anyone else's. Children are already unique in their own fashion, but AS children all focus on different niches. An AS child will learn some college concepts before high school and learn some high school skills in their late 20's. You have an upside-down and sideways child, so accept them even when you can't understand them.

Avoid focusing on the negatives. An AS child has *many* more shortcomings than an NT child, but that child also has more capabilities than an NT. Your child will understand their value from the components you focus on.

Diagnosis/Treatment

Except for *extremely* low functioning autism, all AS children have every capacity to be as "normal" as anyone else. Many AS children grew up to be lawyers, doctors, engineers, and professors. They'll always lag on social skills but will have other non-interpersonal talents and skills that set them apart.

The AS diagnosis is only as useful as you apply it to your parenting style. With the CARS assessment as an example, ignore its general score and focus on the lowest-ranking sections. I've used Appendix A to show you how that would break out.

I hate the implication, but I have no other way to describe it. Treat an AS child like a computer with self-determination. They need well-defined boundaries, a need to organize and create, and full clarification about many, many topics.

Avoid putting an AS child in a special education class. I don't mean anything cruel by it. AS are direct imitators of their environment. An autistic child who only associates with Down's Syndrome and Cerebral Palsy will quickly imitate them. Put them around neurotypical children their age as much as possible. And, more is better. Most of my neurotypical appearance comes from the fact that I've probably met 4,000 people in my life so far.

Vaccines causing AS are probably a complete myth. The fearmongering tied to it has kept it persisting in public discussion. If you're trying to find blame, there is some link between AS and early childhood PTSD. However, since a small child can suffer PTSD over a mere image or sound, you'd have a hard time finding the culprit in our information-inundated society.

Food profoundly affects AS. It may vary on the individual, but science has proven a link between autistic symptoms and too much gluten, sugar, dairy or artificial ingredients. In my opinion, AS suffer a more severe case of the natural hypersensitive reactions to food that *everyone* experiences.

To put bluntly, most AS biomedical procedures like chelation, stem cell therapy, and hyperbaric oxygen are fearmongering. If nobody knows what *causes* AS, how can any of these procedures attack it? If we remove the placebo effect, those techniques may be harming more than helping.

Given the advantages of AS, their diagnosis is an opportunity, *not* a disease or sickness! Your child won't be a copy-paste version of you, but that won't stop them from achieving extreme success!

Environment

Have your child observe as many people as possible. AS children are exceptional imitators and poor improvisers. Enough experience around people will give a framework for appropriate speech and conduct.

One note of caution, though. Try to put your child more around real-life people and media than fiction. Creators magnify fiction, even "based on a true story" movies, for dramatic effect. AS takes things literally, so they can pick up inappropriately extreme behavior from movies, TV, and video games.

You are that child's number one model. Spend quality time with them. They need as much information as possible to compensate for their weak intuition. Your conduct, role, and responsibilities all play a greater part. Consider what you do when they're looking and you're not noticing. They live more by rigid rules about the universe than approximated patterns.

Respect an AS child's desires. This world can stim them very easily and AS children usually develop an intuition for things that trigger an episode. If they refuse something, try to encourage them to try a lighter version of it. AS *must* learn to push against their perceived limits more than NTs. If they don't want to go to the store, let them stay in the car. If they don't like eating vegetables, have them eat only one.

Hardship

Don't shy away from the reality of it. Other kids *will* tease and bully your child. Teach them how to defuse it with humor or redirect the conversation. Be mindful of the words you choose because they will take it literally. There's no easy solution for this, but they must learn valuable skills before "bully" becomes "boss".

Whatever you do, *don't coddle them*! AS have a hard time changing as they grow from children to adults. By treating them as "small adults", they won't have to learn a whole new set of rules for their coming adulthood. Though many parents have issues with this style, it was normal hundreds of years ago for *all* parents. If children have the liberty to explore and experience consequences before their teenage years, they risk short-term injury at the benefit of less long-term pain.

Expect severe challenges ahead for your child that you won't be able to imagine. This will be difficult for you to witness. Tell them how bad it could get but clarify how much potential they have if they can overcome it. Get them to read and watch stories of successes, especially on the spectrum (see Appendix B).

Education

Teach your children all the basic social skills in Appendix C. Get my other book, *How to Stop Looking Autistic*, if you need more detail. The more detail you can specify to them, the better. Instead of saying "wave goodbye!" you should say "move your arm like this to wave!" and specify how. While it takes some adjusting to, remember that they want to learn and just have trouble understanding.

AS children learn at an odd pace. Let them learn as much as they want, but make sure they hit the benchmarks of "adequate" for their lowest subjects. Your child is a prodigy on some subjects, so don't bother with them getting high marks. Nobody cares about good grades as much as you think they do, *especially* in stuff they won't have a career in later. All your child needs to do is pass.

AS behavior in public is a bit like acting. Therefore, if your child feels comfortable with it, get them involved in theater and play productions.

Obsessions

AS children have a manic focus on one thing. That one thing will cycle only on that child's terms. Don't get in the way of it or the child will hate you. If you're concerned about it, sponsor the obsession as far as it's healthy. Again, clarify *why* you're placing that boundary.

Pay close attention to your child's obsession. Search for creative ways to splice that interest into the rest of life, especially toward things you want them to learn. For example, you can *easily* direct Star Wars toward politics, philosophy, religion, energy systems, astronomy, family roles, and computers.

As much as possible, try to direct their obsession toward something meaningful. Usually, healthy interests are productive. Video games are popular, but unhealthy for five hours a day. However, computer programming is a career! Reading comic books can become unhealthy, but not learning how to make science experiments. Watching TV can be unhealthy, but nobody ever has an issue with someone *making* YouTube videos!

Use whatever teaching methods work for them, including Power Cards or YouTube videos. For the most part, good teaching methods won't feel like learning to the student. Nobody hates learning what they like, and the fickleness of AS is no exception!

Maturing

As your child matures, they'll be *quite* educated on whatever they like. Most children outpace their parents on something by age 12, but an AS child likely do it by age 7 or 8! Respect their knowledge and the fact that they've outgrown you on that subject.

When your child is old enough to consider a line of work, inform them that they can do anything they want but be blunt about their legitimate physical limits. Steer them toward technical work that respects people with a low tolerance for risk.

STEM and accounting are great careers for AS. They can compensate for anything with discipline and training. Since AS won't be able to compensate for reflexes, direct them away from any high-reaction work like military infantry or professional sports.

AS try to "set things right" in their desire for normalcy. That desire can transform entire industries. They have the unique ability to ignore how things *feel* and only see how they *are*. Their only battle will be their awkward conduct. Most of them won't even need to study as much as NTs! For all the benefits of AS once trained, read Appendix D.

They'll Make It

As a parent, I can testify to how difficult raising a child is. Compared to an NT child, raising an AS child has more opportunities for success *and* risks of failure!

The diagnosis of AS has spiked the past few years. We don't know much about AS, but parents are still compelled to act. However, parents still have the same job.

Your job is to build the framework for your child to succeed. You're investing in what they'll work with later. AS has more potential for greatness than most AS treatment centers will probably ever communicate. Treat it like ADD: it needs special attention but doesn't have to dictate their life.

Appendix A: CARS Ideas

Relationship to people

Get them around as wide a variety of people as possible

Bring them to new events, public places, and social events

Put them in a social club for something they like

Imitation

Teach them how to imitate and mirror

Play a mirroring game with them

Point out how people behave in public and discuss why they do it

Emotional response

Teach them the correct way to respond to emotions

Put them in front of movies and plays of people expressing or over-expressing feelings

Get them into theater or plays

Body

Use stimulation, meditation, and awareness exercises

Get them outside to play sports or climb trees

Have them dance, teach them dance moves or put them in front of dance video games

Object use

Give them high-reflex video games

Give them a computer like a Raspberry Pi or Arduino

Have them interact with a VR headset or video game with spatial recognition

Get them to play sports

Adaptation to change

Get them outside more

Take them more places

Change small things outside their specific control like bedtime, mealtime, and ordering of things in the common area

Have them read philosophy

Visual response

Expose them to video games that require frequent input

Have them play rhythm games that require direct feedback like Guitar Hero or DDR

Play clapping games or catch with them

Listening response

Play speaking games or the Ungame

Practice conversations with them

Use the speaker/listener technique, where the first person speaks and the second paraphrases until the first person feels heard, then swapping roles

Taste-smell-touch response and use

Use flashcards to draw associations

Teach them to cook

Play association games

Fear and nervousness

Give them stories of successful people

Tell them the legitimate absolute worst-case scenario

Share stories with them of famous AS

Verbal communication

Have frequent conversations with them

Play word association games

Have them use a thesaurus for something they want to say

Non-verbal communication

Play games like Charades

Describe exactly what you mean when you use nonverbals

Ask them what they feel, then show them what that feeling should look like

Activity level

Send them to go outside

Give them tasks to perform

Work out a productivity/to-do system with them

Level and consistency of intellectual response

Ask what they feel

Ask their preferences

Tell them to describe a story, then address the feelings in that story that the characters may have

General impressions

Ask them to summarize an idea

Have them list ideas, then require them to connect all of them without that obvious association

When they use many words, ask for them to paraphrase their idea (i.e., in other words...)

Appendix B: Famous AS

- Hans Christian Andersen
- Dan Aykroyd
- Marty Balin
- Benjamin Banneker (probably)
- Susan Boyle
- Dan Aykroyd
- Tim Burton
- Lewis Carroll
- Henry Cavendish (probably)
- Charles Darwin (probably)
- Tony DeBlois
- Emily Dickinson
- Paul Dirac (probably)
- Albert Einstein (probably)
- Bobby Fischer
- Bill Gates
- Temple Grandin
- Daryl Hannah
- James Hobley
- Thomas Jefferson (probably)
- Steve Jobs
- Linus Torvalds (probably)
- James Joyce (probably)
- Stanley Kubrick
- Courtney Love
- Caiseal Mór

- Wolfgang Amadeus Mozart (probably)
- Michelangelo (probably)
- Isaac Newton (probably)
- Matt Savage
- Jerry Seinfeld
- Satoshi Tajiri
- Nikola Tesla (probably)
- Andy Warhol
- Ludwig Wittgenstein (probably)
- William Butler Yeats (probably)

Appendix C: The Social Rules

I've listed the following social standards that AS must understand. It's not applicable to anyone but AS, but I've placed it here for your convenience. You can read it *far* more in-depth in *How to Stop Looking Autistic*

Hygiene: groomed with no body odor, any perfume or cologne lightly applied

Attire: matches the occasion

Small talk: prepared in advance to compensate, only discussing lightweight inoffensive topics

Greeting: firm but relenting handshake, copy everyone else for greeting and farewell

Mirroring: imitate other people but delay it a bit, don't mirror large gestures

Personal space: only respond to touch, stay 4-12 feet away from people unless it's intimate

Body language: don't fidget, align body with the listener, don't gesture without intent

Facial expressions: Practice thoroughly, make eye contact 85% of the time and mimic NTs, don't stare

Speaking: don't interrupt, make natural speech patterns, only talk about what the other person wants

Respecting limits: play close attention to discomfort cues and honor them, accept when people don't want to talk about something

Appendix D: Socially Skilled AS Advantages

- Detail-minded makes analysis easier when trained
- Niche-mindedness creates opportunities to transform society at the margins
- Easier to recover from hardship because triggers are highly localized to specific circumstances
- Extreme focus and dedication to projects makes highly productive work for long durations
- Neural splinters/savants have unusually exceptional talents that are usually cross-trainable to other disciplines
- Low social interaction allows long hours at a task without human connection
- Need for rhythm and consistency empowers rigorous discipline with clear boundaries
- Obsession with details allows for highly technical work
- Disregard for social standards allows unconventional and creative thought
- Can find meaning in seemingly mundane tasks

Don't miss out!

Visit the website below and you can sign up to receive emails whenever Greg Stucky publishes a new book. There's no charge and no obligation.

https://books2read.com/r/B-A-GYFK-SZJEB

BOOKS2READ

Connecting independent readers to independent writers.

Did you love *How to Start Looking at Autism*? Then you should read *How to Stop Looking Autistic*[1] by Greg Stucky!

[2]

Have you heard of autism and think you have it?Are you on the spectrum and tired of others looking down on you for it?Have you struggled with depression and feel like you'll never make it in public?This guide to autism is written with you in mind.You CAN be normal and CAN succeed with others, and this relatively short book describes exactly how.

Read more at https://stucky.tech.

---

1. https://books2read.com/u/bwvr69

2. https://books2read.com/u/bwvr69

Also by Greg Stucky

Autism
How to Start Looking at Autism
How to Stop Looking Autistic

Philosophy
TL;DR Philosophy

Watch for more at https://stucky.tech.

www.ingramcontent.com/pod-product-compliance
Lightning Source LLC
Chambersburg PA
CBHW031423160726
47993CB00003B/1364